Bibliographic information published by the German National Library:

The German National Library lists this publication in the National Bibliography; detailed bibliographic data are available on the Internet at http://dnb.dnb.de .

Imprint:

Copyright © 2014 GRIN Verlag, Open Publishing GmbH
Print and binding: Books on Demand GmbH, Norderstedt Germany
ISBN: 978-3-668-02078-8

This book at GRIN:

http://www.grin.com/en/e-book/303560/rolling-shutter-bundle-adjustment

Henrique Mendonça

Rolling Shutter Bundle Adjustment

GRIN Publishing

GRIN - Your knowledge has value

Since its foundation in 1998, GRIN has specialized in publishing academic texts by students, college teachers and other academics as e-book and printed book. The website www.grin.com is an ideal platform for presenting term papers, final papers, scientific essays, dissertations and specialist books.

Visit us on the internet:

http://www.grin.com/

http://www.facebook.com/grincom

http://www.twitter.com/grin_com

University of Zurich^{UZH}

Eidgenössische Technische Hochschule Zürich
Swiss Federal Institute of Technology Zurich

Computer Vision
and Geometry Lab

Rolling Shutter Bundle Adjustment

Master's Thesis

Henrique Mendonça
Department of Informatics, UZH

October 23, 2014

Abstract

Rolling shutter cameras are present in virtually every mobile device nowadays and even on high-end cameras. Their line-by-line readout of the image sensors, greatly weakens the assumption of instantaneous exposure made by most computer vision algorithms until recent years. Even short exposure rolling shutter images and videos can exhibit considerable visual distortion when acquired in presence of motion, either from the camera itself or from the scene objects. Traditional structure from motion pipelines have been proven to fail under these conditions, notably in its typical refining step, the bundle adjustment.

Even after over 50 years of research, bundle adjustment is still the state of the art technique for simultaneous optimal estimation of camera poses and scene 3D structure. It has demonstrated its flexibility and robustness over many different kinds of visual models. Nevertheless, handling the extra freedom of the rolling shutter imagery in presence of diverse levels of noise and outliers can be extremely challenging. In this work, we present a very simple and general linear camera model that allows rolling shutters but, at the same time, constrains it to an usable parametrization. We further investigate the amount of information necessary for each level of noise and propose a weak motion prior to additionally constraint the reconstruction.

Contents

Chapter 1

Introduction

Structure-from-motion (SfM) is the estimation of three-dimensional structures from two-dimensional image sequences from one or more cameras, while the camera and/or the scene is moving. The camera motion has to be simultaneously estimated during this process, and it has already found many real world applications. SfM is now commonly used to add visual effects to video, e.g. in the movie industry, TV and augmented reality. It has also been successfully employed to build 3D models from both unordered photo collections and from video.

Until few years ago, virtually all SfM implementations assumed each whole image to be statically and instantaneously captured. This assumption can in fact be close to reality, to a pixel precision, on good quality static pictures taken with a global shutter camera. Cameras fitted with a mechanical shutter or a *charge-coupled device* (CCD) sensor can capture the whole image in a very short period of time – provided correct shutter speed configuration in addition to a static or slow motion scene, and/or with the help of a good optical image stabilization system. However, an overwhelming majority of camera sensors sold today use *complementary metal-oxide-semiconductor* (CMOS) circuits: nearly all mobile video recording devices, compact cameras and, since around 2010, also most high-end *digital single-lens reflex* (DSLR) cameras have them.

In contrast to the classical CCD sensors, the image rows of standard CMOS sensors are read line-by-line in a rapid succession over a readout time of 10-60 ms, depending on refresh rate. This delayed and fragmented image formation is known as an electronic *rolling shutter* (RS). This can lead to a RS camera distortion when combined with motion, of either the camera or the subject. Stretching, squeezing and sharing are common artefacts produced by the RS.

As said before, most work on SfM is based on the global shutter camera model. If classical structure-from-motion is applied to rolling shutter video, the result is unpredictable, as showed by Hedborg et al. [19] and by Saurer et al. [37]. In

1

recent years, many alternative solutions taking RS into consideration appeared in the literature. Very good results were shown and some implementations were even taken to global scale [24]. Meilland et al. [31] also model motion blur together with the RS effects on dense 3D structure, but required a RBG-D input. Apart from the latter and [37], it seems to be no other references handling dense models and RS simultaneously.

Therefore, the objective of the project is to merge some of the current efforts to create a general SfM pipeline, including all its steps, so that it serves as a base for large scale 3D reconstructions. This platform should create a high performance and precise scene reconstruction and camera motion estimation of video input, which can be used to bootstrap denser reconstructions or camera tracking applications. The implementation will focus on dealing the rolling shutter aberrations of commonly available CMOS videos. Nevertheless, the model should be flexible enough to also cope with global shutter video cameras or any ordered set of images.

The estimated camera motion and the SfM sparse 3D model should have precision comparable or superior to other standard methods. For this reason, the work will start by testing popular SfM implementations like Bundler SfM [42], which will serve as a baseline for the further tests. This referred implementation assumes global shutter images, so modeling the rolling shutter should considerably improve the result on video sequences, specially when dealing with relatively fast rotation and translation motions.

1.1 Structure-from-Motion

As mentioned before, SfM is the simultaneous estimation of 3D structure and camera poses. Finding structure-from-motion presents a similar problem as finding three dimensional structure from stereo vision. In both instances, the correspondence between images and the reconstruction of 3D object needs to be found, [7].

To find correspondence between images, 2D features such as corner points (edges with gradients in multiple directions) need to be tracked from one image to the next. The feature trajectories over time are then used to reconstruct their 3D positions and the camera's motion. There is a vast variety of 2D features packages, SIFT [28], SURF [4], ORB [36], KLT [38], etc, which allow the user to extract and track 2D interest points between consecutive images.

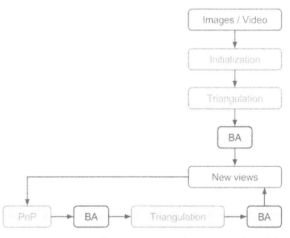

Figure 1.1: Typical structure-from-motion pipeline. Raw data (white boxes) is normally compressed in the form of sparse 2D point features before usage. The blue boxes depict standard methods using epipolar geometry and simpler linear systems to find an initial estimate of the next poses and features. Bundle adjustment BA (red) is used to refine the previous steps to an optimal estimate, normally taking a larger part of the problem into consideration.

Once visual matches were found, they can be used to initialize the reconstruction pipeline as shown on figure 1.1. Epipolar geometry can be used in order to estimate the relative pose between the first two cameras. However, the latter technique cannot be used on the additional images since its pose estimate is up to a scale and conserving the scale between the two independent estimates is not trivial. Nevertheless, the 2D matches can be already triangulated using the first camera pose estimates and their 3D coordinates can be easily used in order to acquire a scale consistent pose estimate for the following images. The latter technique is typically known in the computer vision community as *Perspective-n-Point* (PnP). Figure 1.1 also shows an intermediate *bundle adjustment* (BA) step after each one of the before mentioned steps. BA is a nonlinear refinement step, which can be repeatedly used to improve the estimate, as we see next.

1.2   Bundle Adjustment

Bundle adjustment is the optimal jointly estimate of 3D structure and camera parameters (camera pose and/or calibration). Optimal means that the parameters are refined by minimizing some cost function that quantifies the model fitting error, and jointly that the solution is simultaneously optimal with respect to both structure and camera variations.

The name refers to the *bundles* of light rays tracing from their 3D features to each one of the camera centers, which are optimally *adjusted* with respect to both feature and camera parameters. Equivalently, the whole 3D structure and camera parameters are adjusted together *in one bundle*. Bundle adjustment is simply a large sparse geometric parameter estimation problem, the parameters being the combined 3D feature coordinates, camera intrinsics and extrinsics.

This mathematical method has a long history in the photogrammetry and geodesy literature and has been typically formulated as a nonlinear least squares problem [8, 17, 43, 2, 46]. In computer vision, BA is often used as a refining step in SfM pipelines as it generally requires a reasonably good initialization of the parameterization, specially when working with robust loss functions as we will see in chapter 3.

$$\mathbf{y_n} = \mathbf{KPx_n} \tag{1.1}$$

Classically, a reprojection error is used as the cost function to be optimized. The reprojection of a homogenized 3D feature point x_n is linear and given by the equation 1.1, where P is the perspective transformation from world frame to the camera frame of reference and is composed as a 4x3 matrix $[R|t]$ by the rotation matrix R and a translation vector t. K denotes the camera intrinsics in a 3x3 matrix [18]. The resulting y_n is the reprojection of the keypoint x_n in the image plane in homogeneous coordinates.

Therefore, by assuming a quadratic BA cost function, the solution of the bundle adjustment optimization is at the minimum of the sum of the squared reprojection error as in equation 1.2, where y'_n are the original fixed 2D observations. Since KPx_n uses homogeneous coordinates, a dehomogenizer operator $g : \mathbb{R}^3 \mapsto \mathbb{R}^2$ must be used as defined in equation 1.3. K is normally fixed in a calibrated setup, but can also be jointly optimized with the other parameters P and x_n.

$$\underset{P,x_1,\ldots,x_n}{\operatorname{argmin}} \sum_n \|\mathbf{y'_n} - g(\mathbf{KPx_n})\|^2 \tag{1.2}$$

$$g([x, y, z]') = [\tfrac{x}{z}, \tfrac{y}{z}]' \tag{1.3}$$

As we saw, in a homogenized setup P is composed of a 3x3 rotation matrix and a 3D translation vector. This 3D rotation matrix is obviously over-parametrized as the rotation has only 3 degrees of freedom (DoF). It should be substituted by a lower dimensional parametrization like Euler angles, angle-axis or quaternions. Please note that the latter also suffers from the same problem as its representation includes 4 parameters and Euler angles suffers from the known gimbal locks [39]. Therefore, the angle-axis is the simplest and most direct representation for 3D rotations and has been used in several bundle adjustment setups, including [20, 19, 33, 42, 6].

1.3   Rolling shutter cameras

Rolling shutter cameras are the most common type of digital camera nowadays due to the relative low cost, small size and quality of CMOS sensors. However, they impose an additional difficulty to traditional computer vision techniques. RS cameras captures images not by taking a snapshot of the entire scene at a single instant in time, but rather by quickly scanning across the scene, either horizontally or vertically. Figure 1.2 shows a typical readout sequence of a RS camera with vertical shutter. First, reset signals (blue) are used to clear the scanlines line-by-line. At the same pace, each scanline is read (red and green) after its exposure time. Note that the total frame exposure timing, also called *scanning time*, is considerably larger than the scanline exposure time.

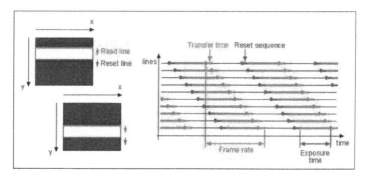

Figure 1.2: Rolling shutter cameras acquire images or video by sequentially re-
seting, exposing and transferring visual data. Source: Matrix Vision

The images obtained during this sequential scanning are equivalent to a instantaneous snapshot, i.e. global shutter (GS), if the camera and scene stay completely static during the whole exposure. However, the sequential exposure of
the images during motion on either sides (camera or scene) will lead to visual
deformations, e.g. stretching, squeezing, smearing or skewing. Figure 1.3 shows
typical visual distortions suffered during camera motion in different directions.

These RS deformations on pictures are seen because all scanlines are generally shown simultaneously, ignoring the fact that they actually represent different points in time. A RS video could potentially be synchronized with a
non-interlaced screen to show the real sequence of the reading. However, this
would have practical implications as the scanning direction and timings can vary
from camera to camera.

This same problem will appear on computer vision techniques, including
structure-from-motion. Holding the global shutter assumption during motion
can easily cause SfM pipelines to fail [20]. The camera's rolling shutter needs
to be taken in consideration in order to correctly estimate the poses and feature
reprojections. However, the full camera model is an underdetermined system as
it would represent 6 DoF per scanline, 3 for translation and 3 for rotation.

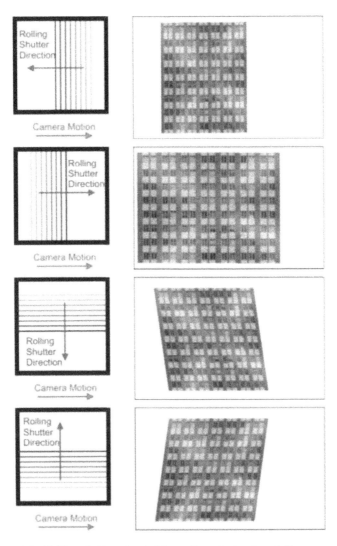

Figure 1.3: Rolling shutter visual deformations during translation movement. Stretching, squeezing or skewing are common in RS images taken in presence of motion. Source: Saurer et al. 2013 [37]

Chapter 2

Structure-from-motion on rolling shutter cameras

As mentioned in the last chapter, independently estimating a pose for every scanline would lead to a very underdetermined system. Nevertheless, coping with rolling shutters is a requirement for any SfM framework which wish to work with nowadays off-the-shelf digital cameras and mobile devices.

There were several publications in recent years that tried to tackle the problematic of the rolling shutter cameras. [24, 19, 33] successfully applied a RS model to the typical bundle adjustment as we will see below. Based on these 3 works we propose a general camera model that can cope with real world datasets, from video to general ordered imagery.

2.1   Related work

2.1.1   Street View Motion-from-Structure-from-Motion, Klingner et al. 2013

Klingner et al. 2013 [24] used RS BA to optimize the position of the car on Google Street View. The data already had very good pose estimates from the in-car GPS/INS system, however, *inertial measurement units* (IMU) are known to drift and GPS localization is not precise, specially in metropolitan areas. Nevertheless, they opted to keep the relative GPS/INS estimate fixed within each image frame of their 15-camera rig and only optimize for the whole car pose at the begin of each aggregated frame (with all 15 cameras).

This setup reduced the freedom of the system back to only 6 DoF like on a GS BA, yet it could explain the motion during exposure by trusting the relatively

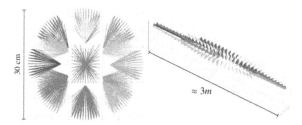

Figure 2.1: Left: Light rays converging to the center of each one of the 15 cameras of the vehicle's rosette, one color per camera. Right: Same rays during typical 30 km/h velocities. Source: Klingner et al. 2013 [24]

good low frequency estimate of the GPS/INS system. This model was successfully used in the Google Street View at a global scale, in spite of that, it relies on high quality GPS/INS hardware, which is not always available. Figure 2.1 depicts their typical camera setup; it clearly shows the position of the scanlines of each camera spreading through over a meter on every shot.

2.1.2 Rolling Shutter Bundle Adjustment, Hedborg et al. 2012

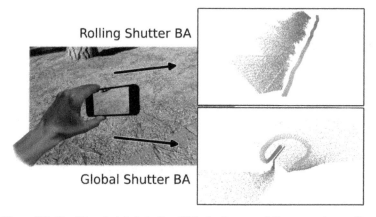

Figure 2.2: Traditional global shutter SfM pipelines can fail on nowadays rolling shutter cameras (bottom right). Source: Hedborg et al. 2012 [19]

Hedborg et al. 2012 [19] creates the first video RS BA as far as we know. They assume a continuous exposure of the sensor and no gaps between frames. Moreover, a linear motion within the exposure time was assumed, interpolating poses between consecutive frames to determinate the position and orientation of each scanline, while also maintaining a system with 6 DoF per frame. Their 6 DoF pose represents the initial scanline of a frame and all the following scanlines are accessed by the interpolation between this initial position and the pose of the next frame. They used linear interpolation for the translation vectors and *spherical linear interpolation* (Slerp) for the rotation.

Additionally to the rolling shutter bundle adjustment step, they also proposed rolling shutter versions of the initialization and PnP step of the SfM pipeline. A rotation only rectification was used on the initialization images before proceeding to the standard methods. Their approach to a general PnP will be discussed in details in section 3.7.

Their setup could successfully model several datasets with natural motion on a smartphone, where the GS SfM pipeline would previously fail as showed on figure 2.2.

2.1.3   Rolling Shutter Camera Calibration, Oth et al. 2013

In order to precisely calculate the line delay, i.e. the time delay between scanlines on a RS video, Oth et al. 2013 [33] elaborated a smooth 4th order B-spline motion model. For this calibration, they used a RS BA to fit the model on videos of a known structure, which is partially equivalent to a SfM pipeline.

However, in order to have an estimate of high precision they iteratively repeat the process to also estimate the optimal knot placement on the B-spline curve. This latter process is not only extremely time demanding but it could potentially lead to overfitting, as showed by themselves in figure 2.3. We strongly believe this problem would show itself even more heavily on noisy environments, where the position of the 3D points is not known and cannot be precisely estimated.

2.2   Proposed model

In this work, we model a general camera which can cope in a transparent way not only with global shutters, but also with the most common rolling shutters digital cameras. This model should be able to incorporate the extra degrees of freedom

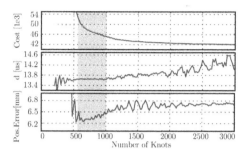

Figure 2.3: Although the uniform B-spline knot placement continuously reduces the reprojection error as more knots are used (top), the camera position estimate error (bottom) and the deviation in their line delay prediction (middle) start increasing again after a certain point. This indicates overfitting to the noisy data on the right side of the grayed out area. Source: Oth et al. 2013 [33]

caused by the sequential readouts without overparameterizing the system.

As reported earlier [33], most video cameras do have an additional delay between consecutive frames. Additionally, we would like to also be able to work with non-video datasets of ordered but more spaced out images, similar to Google Street View data [24] without requiring any non-visual information. For these datasets, the RS BA proposed by Hedborg et al. [19] might not be the best fit because of their assumption that the pose of the first scanline in a frame is the same as the last scanline in the previous frame. The latter model would not be able to explain the large gap between frame acquisitions without compromising the pose estimation.

Therefore, we propose a model with additional freedom for noncontinuous sets of images. Like Hedborg et al. [19], we assume a linear motion of continuous velocity within a single image frame, as the exposure time does not normally exceed a couple of tens of milliseconds – around 30ms on modern smart phones [33]. This linear motion can be easily represented by the position and orientation of the first and last scanlines of each frame, in a total of 12 DoF, i.e. 3 DoF for position and another 3 for orientation at the first scanline pose, and the same again for the last scanline. As we assume a constant linear motion throughout the frame exposure time, the intermediate poses can be found by a linear interpolation between the two extremes.

We will go into more details on the whole proposed RS pipeline in the next chapter, and specifically on the latter model in section 3.5.

Chapter 3

SfM Pipeline

Bundle adjustment is really just a refining step and cannot be used as a standalone solution to the pose and structure estimation problem. As any other least squares optimization, it strongly depends on a *reasonable* initialization [44]. Reasonable, in the visual bundle adjustment perspective, does not necessarily mean something extremely close to the optimal solution, instead, it generally only requires estimate to lie on valid a position and orientation. This latter can mean that light ray should point to the correct direction, i.e. the 3D feature points should be in front of each camera which happens to see it. Still, even completely wrong camera poses can be corrected if good data is provided and enough trust is put on them, e.g. by fixing the already estimated 3D feature points. Therefore, the optimization system is also extremely dependent on the quality of the data and outliers configuration, as we will see later.

A good camera pose initialization can also be used for direct outlier screening, by removing the visual features with higher reprojection error, and therefore increasing the overall data consistency. This again requires a certain degree of trust on the initial estimates. Nevertheless, traditional and openly available methods for camera pose estimate, like the 8-point algorithm and PnP [18], have been already used for many years and offer very good and robust results for GS imagery. This situation is a bit different for RS cameras, since there are still a lack of methods specifically designed for them and none covers all motion aspects of these cameras [19]. However, as we mentioned before, the total frame exposure (scanning time) of the RS cameras is generally short, and very large motions during this period would result in unusable blurry images.

Therefore, the before mentioned GS methods should still be of use for a initial estimate, as we can assume that the motion during the image exposure is small enough to approximated to GS for an initial guess. This assumption is in fact usable in real world datasets [33] and can be used to bootstrap the RS BA as it will be showed later in the next chapter.

With all this in hand, we can now propose a RS SfM pipeline which should be able to successfully reconstruct the 3D scene and at the same time estimate the camera poses during the sequence, including the motion within each image exposure time. We will be focusing here only on ordered sequences of images and videos. These kinds of datasets provide important information about the relation between consecutive frames, which will be used to efficiently track the visual components of the scene throughout the whole sequence. Although this pipeline is rolling shutter aware, it should not be necessary to add any extra step to the regular SfM pipeline as showed on figure 1.1. In our pipeline the red bundle adjustment boxes are substituted by the RS BA with the proposed model, which is capable of correcting the initial assumption and estimate the motion within the frame exposure timing. In following sections, we will go through all the pipeline steps including the pre-processing steps of feature extraction and matching, which are required before the new views are added to the sequence.

3.1   Feature extraction

Although, there are works in the literature showing good results on extracting structure from visual lines [3], curves [34] or direct image correlation [30], it is almost a consensus nowadays for using 2D interest points. There are several available packages for extracting and matching 2D features, and most were proved very robust to scale, rotation and affine distortions. For the rest of the work we will only use SIFT [28] for the its long tradition in the computer vision community, but mostly because the choice of feature should be irrelevant to the general result of the tests on real data. After extraction, all descriptors are serialized [41] and stored, so the process does not need to be repeated for multiple matchings.

3.2   Feature matching

Generally most SfM pipelines try to match all features of all images against all other ones and rank the matches to find the closest image pairs and next images to process. This is a computer intensive process with quadratic complexity in the number of images and features, if a simple brute force matching is used.

Since we are mainly targeting ordered sequences of images and videos, it is obvious that consecutive frames should have similar features, and therefore, should be matched. In all real data tests presented in this work, we match the current working frame with the previous 5 frames and assume there is enough overlap between them. This number could be adjusted to improve performance or quantity of matches, yet it does not seem to have great impact on the final result and is out of the scope of this project.

Please note that to prove the possibility of using the pipeline on a real life running system, we will process the frames in a filter like way, and only add new frames to existing data by matching its features to already processed ones. However, we do not take any previous pose estimate in consideration and always try to match every feature descriptor in a frame with every other descriptor in the previous frames. In this way, we will not require reprocessing frames multiple times and can completely separate the pre-processing from the rest of the pipeline.

We perform a single way nearest-neighbor matching between the current and each one of the 5 last seen frames, with a Lowe threshold of 0.85 [28] to avoid problems with visually repetitive features. Moreover, additional features are eliminated when their 2D distance between the two matching frames is more than twice as large as the average. This automatically rejects outliers that will have large reprojection errors later on.

Like in the feature extraction, these matches against all 5 previously processed frames are serialized and stored for further use.

3.3 Feature tracking

The matches between 2D features of different image frames can be combined to create *tracks*. We will name a *track* the set of reprojections of a single 3D feature point in a series of images or video frames. Establishing tracks from pairs of matches in a noise-free and non-redundant environment is a straight forward task, even without knowing the intrinsic 3D point. However, in presence of outliers or repetitive visual features, it is impossible to distinguish between good and bad configurations only with visual information [28]. The tracks might end up branching into different directions for every distinct pair of images that were matched.

In order to restrict our tracks to one single consistent and realistic layout we limit to one reprojection per 3D feature point on each image frame. By using the current best pose estimate, we choose the visual match with the lowest reprojection error. The process will be repeated after every change on the pose estimates so that new tracks can be formed or existing ones extended with now valid new reprojections. This require us to trust the pose estimate in order to improve it with more visual information, which goes along with the idea of BA as a refining step.

Together with pose estimation itself, the process of alternating between visual information acquisition and pose estimate can be compared to the visual-geometric fusion achieved with semi-direct methods like [22] or [15]. However, in the proposed pipeline we are restricting ourselves to already extracted interest points with known good visual parity. Please also note that KLT tracking [38] also offers an equivalent solution, with the additional assumption that the movement between frames is small enough to be close to zero. KLT can offer a very robust and computational cheap tracking for high frequency and slow motion videos but the latter assumption will not hold for real datasets similar to Google Street View or any video with faster motion.

3.3.1   Triangulation

Our structure reconstruction is done by a simple 2-view triangulation to take advantage of the sequential processing of the imagery. The resulting 3D point is reprojected to all visually matching frames for a geometric confirmation, including the latter two used in the triangulation. A pixel threshold of 3 pixels is used in this case to allow the new frames to create a new track or to be added to an existing one. Only tracks containing at least 3 valid reprojections are used in the further refining steps. This pixel threshold is equivalent to an angular threshold, therefore each one of the selected features have a 3D error distribution area proportionally bound to their distance to the camera center, i.e. features far from the viewer may have larger 3D errors than close ones.

3.4   GS initialization

Once good visual matches were found between the first two images of the reconstruction, standard algorithms can be used to give us a first pose estimate [18]. In this framework, we use the open source set of computer vision tools provided by OpenCV [6] to robustly extract the fundamental matrix through random sample consensus (RANSAC) [13]. We assume the initial camera pose to be at origin. The best GS pose estimate for the second image can be easily assessed from the 4 possible solutions derived from the essential matrix [18, chap.9] as we assume a calibrated setup, i.e. camera intrinsic parameters (such as focal length, principal points) have been previously calibrated.

3.4.1 RS correction

As we will discuss later in the next chapter, the additional freedom of the rolling shutter pose makes its estimate extremely vulnerable to outliers. Since it is hard to guarantee a proper outlier screening without knowing the correct poses and motion pattern, we propose to keep a GS initialization until a better method is developed, rather than using an approximation of any form, as in [19]. This proposal requires a RS video sequence to begin with static GS frames but this still practicable in real life by simply starting a reconstruction with two images in a static setup. This initialization would yield precise as possible 3D points, which the reprojection can then be used to constrain the following RS poses. However, the two view initialization itself does not generally provide enough constrains to allow a RS correction in a noisy real world setup, and this explains the initial requirement for static imagery.

3.5 Rolling shutter bundle adjustment

In section 2.2, we briefly explained our proposal for a general camera model which is able to model both global and rolling shutter cameras. We assume a linear motion of constant velocity between the begin and end of the image exposure time. This assumption holds true for all tested synthetic and real life datasets, since the exposure time is quite short in most nowadays digital cameras [23].

The reprojection model of a rolling shutter camera is similar to the global shutter model given by equation 1.1. However, in the general camera, scanlines are read sequentially and in distinct times. Consequently, each scanline might have a different and independent camera pose, as showed in equation 3.1. Where P_l represents the camera pose at scan time for each line or row of the image, for vertical and horizontal rolling shutter respectively. Note that the nonlinear lens distortion $d(.)$ [21] cannot be corrected in advance because the rolling shutter readout happens on the optically distorted image. Pre-rectifying the frames to this lens distortion would alter the images coordinates and cause loss of information about the scanning sequence. We used 3 radial and 2 tangential parameters for our distortion model, which is compatible with standard OpenCV library.

$$\mathbf{y_{n,t}} = \mathbf{K}d(\mathbf{P_t x_n}) \tag{3.1}$$

Assuming a linear motion within the frame exposure time reduces the parametrization of the frame poses to a total of 12 DoF, as all intermediate poses can be acquired from the linear interpolation of the first and last positions – with 6 DoF each. Therefore, P_t is the perspective transformation matrix for one scanline read in time t. P_t is the result from the linear interpolation between the first and last scanlines of every frame, respectively parametrized by the 6D vectors p_{first} and p_{last}. These 6D vectors are composed by stacking their 3D angle-axis vector on top of the translation vector.

Consequently, P_t is a function of p_t and its rotation component can be calculated with the Rodrigues' rotation formula [5]. The direct linear interpolation is given by the equation 3.2a, where $\tau_t \in [0, 1]$ and can be determined from the original scanline index of the image, as in equation 3.2b assuming a horizontal left-to-right rolling shutter for simplicity. Here, u is the horizontal coordinate of the 2D image and v should be used instead for a vertical RS, e.g. $\tau_t = 1 - \frac{v_t}{v_{max}}$ for a bottom-to-top shutter. This general model can also be used on global shutter data. In this case, the first and last poses are equal.

$$\mathbf{p_t} = \mathbf{p}_{first} + \tau_t(\mathbf{p}_{last} - \mathbf{p}_{first}) \tag{3.2a}$$

$$\tau_t = \frac{\mathbf{u_t}}{\mathbf{u_{max}}} \tag{3.2b}$$

For the rolling shutter bundle adjustment, we again assume a quadratic error function, where the error is the difference between the reprojected 3D feature points and the original observations. Therefore, the solution of the optimization are the arguments of the minimum sum of the squared reprojection errors of all 3D points, as showed in 3.3

$$\operatorname*{argmin}_{P_1,\dots,P_t,x_1,\dots,x_n} \sum_t \sum_n \|\mathbf{y'_{n,t}} - g(\mathbf{K}d(\mathbf{P_t x_n}))\|^2 \tag{3.3}$$

The current framework makes use of the Ceres Solver [1] open source library for solving the nonlinear least squares problems on every BA step of the pipeline. The default bundle adjustment options were used, i.e. the standard LevenbergMarquardt algorithm with a sparse Schur decomposition, auto-differentiation and Huber loss as the robust loss function. There are possible options to improve performance but we will not cover this here.

3.6   Interpolation of the angle-axis vector

A careful reader might have noticed that we are directly and linearly interpolating the angle-axis vector. Its known that angle-axis vectors do not obey regular vector operations, including the used addition and subtraction. Consequently, direct interpolating the rotation vector is not necessarily mathematically sound, in spite of that, for small angles it shows itself numerically equivalent to the widely used spherical linear interpolation (Slerp) proposed by Shoemake already in 1985 [39].

3.6.1   Slerp & NLerp

Slerp [39] was introduced in the context of quaternion interpolation for the purpose of animating 3D rotation in computer graphics. It interpolates between two given quaternions to a constant-speed motion along a unit-radius great circle arc and guarantees the torque-minimal path. However, it requires multiple additional nonlinear function calls per evaluation, which can greatly increase the computational cost of the BA reprojections as the interpolation must be calculated for every single 3D point reprojection. Together with the conversions from angle-axis to quaternions and back, these operations alone are several times more computationally expensive than the reprojection function itself.

The normalized linear interpolation (NLerp), also mentioned by Shoemake [39], is also a widely used alternative. Very similar to 3.2a, the linear interpolation is given by $q_\tau = q_0 + \tau(q_1 - q_0)$, yet normalized quaternions are used here. This method is already a great improvement in performance but the conversions between angle-axis and normalized quaternions representations are still necessary for the optimization. The latter conversions represent about half of the cost of the total Slerp from angle-axis. Furthermore, NLerp does not maintain constant velocity during the interpolation path, which breaks our assumption of continuous motion.

3.6.2   Angle-axis vector interpolation

Empirical experiments show that directly interpolating the angle-axis vector is numerically equivalent to the optimal Slerp for small rotations. In practice, larger angles are not commonly found in vision as they would result in extreme image blur, nonetheless, for completeness the used interpolation would still result in non-optimal but possible trajectory. Although the resulting trajectory might not be optimal, nothing guarantees that the torque-minimal path from Slerp should better fit real life data. Figure 3.1 shows large rotation trajectories in the unit sphere around the camera center for both Slerp (red) and the direct angle-axis interpolation (yellow).

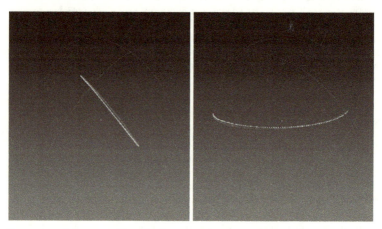

Figure 3.1: Comparing Slerp (red) and angle-axis vector interpolation (yellow). The camera center is shown as the light blue dot and the traced line depicts the center of the image frame, interpolated between the two different orientations vectors. The initial and final orientations are separated by approximately 1 radian on the left and 3 on the right.

Thus, the simple direct linear interpolation offers a good approximation to Slerp for small deviations between initial and end interpolation vectors. Its efficiency and simplicity is ideal for auto-differentiation and/or large scale problems. A extra care has to be taken with the rotation singularity at $2k\pi$, since no additional check is taken to verify the poses consistency. This singularity issue is also mentioned by Oth et al. [33, section 4.1] and showed in figure 3.2 (right).

3.7   Least Squares RS PnP

Bundle adjustment is used to refine the joint pose and structure estimate, after the initialization and triangulation of the visually and geometrically consistent matches. The resulting 3D feature points can be used to add additional views to reconstruction, this method is known in the computer vision community as Perspective-n-Point. The minimal parametrization and efficient closed form solution is given by Perspective-3-Point [16] for global shutter cameras.

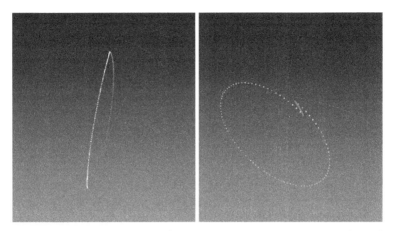

Figure 3.2: Comparing Slerp (red) and angle-axis vector interpolation (yellow) like in figure 3.1. Linearly interpolating the angle-axis vectors might not be optimal for certain rotations, i.e. it might not give the shortest path between two orientations. The right interpolation shows a predictable result when the norm of the vectors difference is above π.

An alternative solution, also widely used and also available in OpenCV, is the Levenberg-Marquardt optimization minimizing the reprojection error like in equation 1.2. However, in this case the 3D points x_n are assumed to be optimal and fixed. This reduces the freedom of the system and can find good estimates even without any prior knowledge of the camera pose, which is necessary for the full BA. The latter method can use more points, compensating for small Gaussian noise, but can fail in the presence of non-gaussian outliers and cannot be used in practice without a RANSAC approach.

$$\underset{P_{t+1},\ldots,P_{t+k}}{\operatorname{argmin}} \sum_{i=1}^{k}\sum_{j=1}^{n} \|\mathbf{y'_{i,j}} - \mathbf{d}(\mathbf{KP_{t+i}x_j})\|^2 \tag{3.4}$$

Hedborg et al. [19] proposed to extend this initial optimization problem for their rolling shutter model, and also used it to simultaneously estimate multiple new frame poses on their video datasets. As mentioned before, the implementation for such a problem is very similar the general bundle adjustment and it is given by equation 3.4 for k new poses. However, it provides very limited robust-

ness against outliers and can badly fail for more sparse datasets, and specially
with the additional degrees of freedom of our proposed camera model. We will
see experimental results in the next chapter and figure 4.8 where the method fails
even with a small percentage of outliers – much larger ratios are to be expected
in real life datasets. In this case, the two independent 6 DoF poses tend to accumulate errors proportional to the noise levels and their estimates may diverge.
As we discussed before, the KLT method used by Hedborg et al. provides an additional geometric validation on the visual matches by assuming similar camera
poses during consecutive video frames and 2D proximity in the image plane. Because of KLT, their pipeline is free of large outliers but these assumptions cannot
be hold true in datasets with larger motions, preventing a better outliers filtering.

Consequently, similarly to the GS initialization we propose to use proven GS
methods for the first estimate of a new pose. A GS PnP estimate is accept-
able as a first approximation since we assume that the camera movement to be
small within the total image readout time. RANSAC is again the best practice
for the acquisition of an estimate robust to outliers of any distribution. However, the reprojection error threshold of the RANSAC outlier screening has to
be accordingly adjusted, in a similar way as KLT has to be adjusted to possible
inter-frame movement. We use here the double of the pixel threshold used in the
feature tracking. A optimal threshold could actually be calculated in accordance
to the known 3D structure and the predicted intra-frame motion but this will be
left as a possible future extension or might not be necessary at all as we will see
next.

The GS estimate returned by the RANSAC PnP can be used to bootstrap
the RS least squares optimization. Most wrong matches and other larger outliers can be eliminated by trusting this prior up to a threshold as mentioned
above. The optimal RS pose can be estimated by minimizing equation 3.4, even
in the presence of some Gaussian noise as we will see next in figure 4.7. It will
be demonstrated in the next chapter how this procedure yields good results on
synthetic and real world data.

Note that these two steps, GS PnP and RS correction, do not necessarily need
to be kept separated and a possible *RANSAC RS PnP* will be discussed in chapter 5. In this proposed RS PnP, the RANSAC pixel threshold is only dependent
on the precision of the feature detection itself and therefore independent of any
inter-frame motion.

3.7.1 Motion priors

Robust operators and loss functions, like Huber norm, model the scene as perfectly normally distributed inliers with uniformly distributed outliers. However, the 2D images and their features are nothing more than a limited sample of that, where distributions are way less than perfect. Moreover, SIFT and other point features can suffer from unmodeled distortions on complex 3D structure with partial occlusions and visual redundancies. Again, the additional freedom of the general model can try to explain these error aberrations by moving the camera poses to unrealistic positions, while still satisfying a good reprojection of the remaining features. By observing the camera pose reconstruction, one can easily tell whether the estimated pose is plausible or not due to the physical constraints of real cameras. This means the trajectory of a camera in a video sequence cannot be completely different from a frame to the next. Generally a constant velocity or acceleration model is assumed for real world hand-held cameras [11].

We can further constraint our model in order to get a more consistent and realistic reconstruction by taking advantage of prior knowledge on how videos are shot. As we will see on the next chapter, a simple constant velocity model already fits well trajectories like of a driving car. Even a weak prior can already help keeping a consistent trajectory when visual information is less available or not enough geometrically constrained. Such model can be easily constructed by simply calculating the velocity in the given point in time directly before the current measurement like in equation 3.5b, where p_{i-1} and p_{i-2} are any two previous poses respectively at times t_{i-1} and t_{i-2}. The current velocity should then be equal to the former, i.e. $v_i \overset{!}{=} v_{i-1}$. As p_i is the stacked 6D parametrization of the current pose, 3D angle-axis on top of the 3D translation vector, this model also includes the approximated angular velocities.

$$\delta_{i-1} = t_{i-1} - t_{i-2} \tag{3.5a}$$

$$v_{i-1} = \frac{p_{i-1} - p_{i-2}}{\delta_{i-1}} \tag{3.5b}$$

The rolling shutter cameras simplify this in the way that we can calculate not only the velocity between frames but also within the frame itself. In this case, δ_{i-1} is the inter-frame delay and δ_i the frame scanning time, i.e. the time between the first and last scanlines. The velocity during the image scanning is then given by $\frac{p_i - p_{i-1}}{\delta_i}$. However, in the general case it is possible that $\delta_i = 0$ as t_i could be equal to t_{i-1}, i.e. a global shutter frame, which would result in an infinite velocity.

An alternative solution is to use the same model to predict the current position, as given by equation 3.6a. This assumes zero acceleration and therefore the same constant velocity. Note that in case of $\delta_i = 0$, the prediction p_i is equal to p_{i-1}, hence a global shutter camera. The same equation 3.6a is also used to predict the inter-frame delay by calculating p_{i-1} with its equivalent equation $p_{i-1} = p_{i-2} + v_{i-2}\delta_{i-1}$ but it will be omitted here for simplicity.

$$p_i = p_{i-1} + v_{i-1}\delta_i \tag{3.6a}$$

$$e = p_i - p_i' \tag{3.6b}$$

In BA, the cost function 3.6b is called a *prior* with residual e. It can be transparently added to the optimization problem and jointly solved with the re-projection cost function and any other priors. Please also note that the timings between and within the frames do not necessarily needed to be known, as all calculation listed above can be done instead by using a ratio between the two timings. This ratio $d = \frac{\delta_i}{\delta_{i-1}}$ is constant, if both timings are assumed to not change throughout the video sequence.

Similarly, a constant acceleration model can be constructed from a higher order model given by the equations 3.7. This model will fit better the changes of velocity, very common in real world data. Higher order models could be also used instead, reinforcing constant jerk, or even jounce. However, these models would require more data, i.e. additional frame poses in the past, in order to estimate their parametrization. This could create an additional pressure on smoothing the trajectory, and its consequences on data with fast motion is not competently clear. Further comparative tests with more precise data would be required for a better evaluation.

$$p_i = p_{i-1} + v_{i-1}\delta_i + \frac{a_{i-1}\delta_i^2}{2} \tag{3.7a}$$

$$a_{i-1} = \frac{v_{i-1} - v_{i-2}}{\delta_{i-1}} \tag{3.7b}$$

Chapter 4

Experiments

The proposed pipeline was evaluated on several real world and synthetic datasets. It was not only able to successfully reconstruct global shutter data but also imagery from everyday rolling shutter cameras, where traditional pipelines would fail. Next in this chapter, we will show the specific cases where the proposed general camera model must replace the assumption of instantaneous image acquisition, as well as the drawbacks this model has in certain circumstances in relation to the tradition techniques.

4.1 Improving GPS/INS prior

Google Street View imagery is tightly coupled with the high quality vehicular GPS/INS system of the car that was used to run the cities and produce its data. To recap, Klingner et al. [24] used this data to optimally estimate the car trajectory within Google Maps. They trusted the high frequency prior estimate and only optimized for the general pose of the car at one single point in time per shot – therefore 6 DoF for each 15-camera 360-degree panorama – maintaining the relative pose of the scanlines in relation to the car accordingly with the initial GPS/INS prior.

To simulate a vision only setup we use the GPS/INS data just as initialization and bundle adjust the poses using the general camera model from section 3.5. Our initialization only uses their first and last scanline poses to set our 12 DoF model for one single camera, and not all 1944 available scanline poses per camera, reducing our dependency on a high frequency hardware while testing the fitness of our linear motion assumption. This is a good test for the whole pipeline as it is known that the pose optimization should converge to something close to initial estimate due to its high quality. It also allow us to check the implementation of the feature extraction, matching, tracking and bundle adjustment itself on a simple single-camera environment.

Although the vehicles were provided with high quality GPS/INS hardware, inertial systems are known for their highly noisy low frequency output and GPS is of little use for this scale of precision. Therefore, most systems employ high-pass filters to smooth and remove high frequency noise from the data. However, at the same time, they also filter out high frequency motion information, which could be useful to RS reconstruction. Moreover, the integration of accelerometer data can accumulate small measurement errors resulting in drift, which can also only be corrected up to the GPS precision. Hence there must be some space for improvement on the prior estimate.

Figure 4.1: Dense RS stereo-vision depth-maps [37] fused into one 3D reconstruction.

4.1.1 Effects on dense reconstructions

One of the goals of this work was to create precise camera and structure estimate in order to bootstrap dense reconstructions. In 2013, Saurer et al. [37] developed a rolling shutter aware stereo vision algorithm to produce dense 3D reconstructions. However, their plane sweep stereo relies strongly on the correct pose of the cameras, which cannot be precisely retrieved on real world applications without external motion capture systems. Their algorithm performed well on synthetic data but could not create precise reconstructions on datasets like the Google Street View.

As we discussed before, GPS/INS can give a very good pose estimate but drift and other small errors are to be expected. It is still possible to run their plane sweep algorithm on Google's Street View data, and the results look quite good at a first glance. The reconstructed depth-maps are created from each image and their visual correspondences in the closest 4 neighbors and then jointly displayed in the same model. Figure 4.1 demonstrates the reconstruction of the San Francisco City Hall, which look reasonable from the front view. However, even

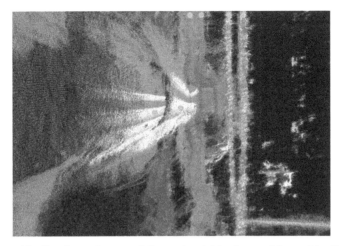

Figure 4.2: Top down close-up of the center right column of figure 4.1. Green markings show misaligned structures due to wrong GPS/INS poses.

Figure 4.3: Dense RS stereo-vision depth-maps [37] fused into one 3D reconstruction using RS BA poses and weak constant acceleration prior. Shows considerable improvement in comparison to the original prior estimate used in figure 4.2.

small errors on the pose estimate can create large misalignments in the integrated model. The typical structural distortion caused by these errors is seen from a bird's eye view on image 4.2. The front wall and columns are shown in distinct positions in different depth-maps, which causes the impression of "double walls". After our proposed RS BA these poses are more consistent and the depth-maps match each other on a single reconstruction. The result is still noisy but the points are distributed in tightly overlapping clouds as seen on figure 4.3.

4.2   Measurements on synthetic data

In order to precisely benchmark the result of the proposed RS BA, we created a simple synthetic setup with known 3D structure and camera poses. This allows us to further analyze the influence of noise and motion levels on the final results.

Figure 4.4: A GS camera traversing in front of the cube of uniformly distributed features. The red points represent the camera centers and the yellow point indicates the orientation of that camera by drawing a point on the optical axis 1 meter in front of the camera center.

A random cube of uniformly distributed synthetic 3D feature points was created with an edge dimension of 10 meters. The test camera takes a linear trajectory in front of this cube with constant spacial and angular velocity while keeping its orientation approximately in direction to the center of the cube. The initial and final poses are upright cameras directed to the center of the features, and the orientations of the intermediate cameras are a spherical linear interpolation (Slerp) of these two. The maximal distance between the cameras and the center

Figure 4.5: A RS camera moves linearly through the same trajectory in from of the feature cube as in figure 4.4. The line segments transitioning from blue to green show the sequential camera center positions during the exposure, again the yellow lines represent the respective camera's viewing direction. In this configuration the camera moves 1 meter during each frame exposure period.

of the cube is of 9 meters, which gives a mean scene depth for the reprojections of also about 9 meters. We can then vary the total displacement during exposure to simulate the RS effect to varied velocities levels. Additionally, small levels of white noise can be added to the reprojections of the 3D points onto the synthetic images to simulate a noisy feature detection. The camera setup with zero displacement GS sequence is shown in figure 4.4 and a 1 meter RS exposure in figure 4.5. While 4.6 represents the reprojections of these 3D points on the respective first cameras of these two experiments.

4.2.1 Influence of noise/outliers

As we discussed in the last chapter, the estimation problem of a GS pose consists of 6 unknowns, 3 for orientation and 3 for position. In the case of a RS camera we have the 3 unknowns for position and 3 for orientation, but also 3 for intra-frame velocity and another 3 for intra-frame rotation. This extra 6 degrees of freedom (DoF) of the proposed model – in a total of 12 DoF – will require more information for its estimation. In a noise free environment, 3 distinct 3D points are enough to estimate a GS pose, therefore, 6 points should be enough to predict the 12 DoF of a RS camera. However, this number is a lot less clear when working in presence of noise and specially outliers. Figure 4.7 and 4.8 show the average error and standard deviation of the camera pose estimate on

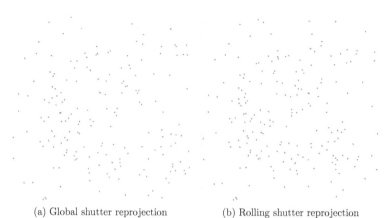

(a) Global shutter reprojection   (b) Rolling shutter reprojection

Figure 4.6: (a) GS reprojection of camera 1 in figure 4.4 with additional white noise. (b) RS reprojection of camera 1 in figure 4.5 with its 1 meter displacement during exposure. In addition to the apparent squishing on the RS image (right), the 2D configuration is slightly altered as points closer to the camera will be displaced farther.

global shutter data, i.e. with no movement during exposure. The poses are initialized already with the correct parameters, but the 2D reprojections have added increasing white noise or uniformly distributed outliers instead of the correct reprojection. The displayed results are gathered after convergence of the bundle adjustment iterations using the 6 DoF GS camera model (blue) and our proposed 12 DoF general model (green). We limit the maximum BA iteration count to 50 but convergence is normally achieved within 5 to 10 iterations on low error setups.

The *average rotation error* is the arithmetic mean sum of absolute differences (SAD) of the Euler angles over all scanlines and all cameras, normalizing one camera at a time. This means that one camera is set as reference, then the SAD error of the Euler angles of all other cameras is computed relative to the reference camera. The same is repeated for every camera, setting it as a reference and calculating the error for the others. The mean SAD for all cameras and their scanlines is then calculated and the average value of all reference poses is used.

Obviously, the results of our model are much worst in this circumstances due to its additional 6 DoF, unnecessary for this GS dataset. Note that in this situation, the initial and final poses of each RS camera should remain the same after BA, and this is true in noise free environments. Yet the two poses of each image

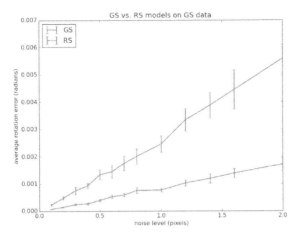

Figure 4.7: The proposed 12 DoF general model should show the same pose for both initial and final parameters on GS data. However, the additional degrees of freedom makes it about 3 times more susceptible to noise than the traditional 6 DoF GS BA.

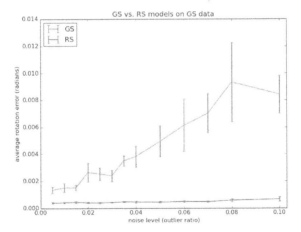

Figure 4.8: Similar to susceptibility to noise showed on fig. 4.7, the proposed RS BA can fail badly in the presence of uniformly distributed outliers, even with the use of a robust loss function.

Figure 4.9: Noisy and poor data can cause the RS BA to converge to an incorrect configuration. The estimated camera trajectory constantly change its orientation, and is far from the ground truth linear motion depicted in figure 4.5.

tend to show different and incorrect configurations in order to explain the noise and outliers from the 2D images. Figure 4.9 pictures a typical inaccurate pose estimate originating from RS BA on noisy synthetic imagery. Please note that a very reduced amount of 3D feature points were used to produce such an incorrect pose estimate. As a matter of fact, the quantity of information available is almost as important as its quality. We can see in figure 4.10 different amounts of 3D points can strongly influence the quality of the estimate.

However, because we know the physical properties of the reconstructed camera trajectory, a much smoother path is to be expected. In section 3.7.1, we have seen that weak motion priors are a simple way to introduce this *a priori* knowledge into the optimization problem. Although the simple GS camera model seems to work better on the previous dataset, the results look considerably different when in presence of even low velocities. Figure 4.11 shows how the GS model degrades as the motion during exposure increases, as well as how a weak acceleration prior (red) can also help to further constrain the model. The horizontal axis indicates the translation motion in meters but proportional rotation is also present as the camera keeps its orientation towards the center of the features, section 4.2. This yaw rotation is of approximately 4.4 degrees per meter of translation.

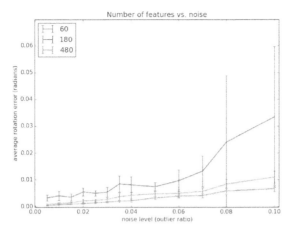

Figure 4.10: 60, 180 and 480 3D points were used to estimate the 5 RS frames with increasing outlier ratio up to 10%. Larger quantities of data can compensate for its low caliber. RS BA can be very susceptible to noise and outliers without enough redundant and well distributed data.

4.3 Full pipeline

The analysis of the results on bundle adjusting GS and RS data suggests that correct estimate of the camera motion is indispensable even under only moderate velocities. No trustworthy estimate of the 3D structure and camera position can be made without considering the sequential readouts of the rolling shutters when in presence of motion. Nevertheless, the proposed pipeline can use the RS BA refining step to extend standard GS computer vision algorithms to a general and RS aware camera model. Although a good initial guess of the parameters is a crucial point on BA, the GS pose showed itself to be enough to bootstrap a precise RS estimate when working with fixed 3D feature points. The complete joint optimization of the 3D structure and camera poses does not seem to be possible without the presence of several views from different angles in order to constrain the feature position. This precise number of necessary views possibly highly depends again on the noise level of the visual features being used and the geographic configuration of the cameras.

Until a full-RS initialization method is developed we will assume a good 3D initial structure estimate. This is still achievable in reality by using GS imagery for the first poses, as mentioned on section 3.4.1. In order to test this proposal

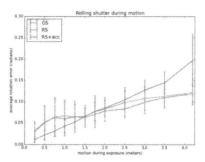

(a) Camera pose average rotation error in radians for increasing motion during exposure.

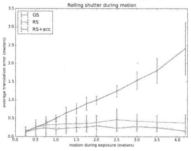

(b) Camera pose translation error in meters for increasing motion during exposure.

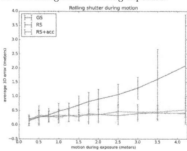

(c) Average 3D point position error in meters for increasing motion during exposure.

Figure 4.11: Average structure and camera pose estimate error during motion of varied levels. 0.7 pixel white noise was used on the 2D reprojections of 100 point features on 5 cameras. GS BA (blue) shows much larger errors even with relatively small displacements during image exposure, in special for the 3D structure estimate. A weak acceleration prior (red) can also help restraining the effects of noise on the RS BA (green).

we use texturized synthetically generated GS and RS images with known poses. The dataset was originally captured from a 3D laser scan [37]. The resulting 3D point cloud has been smoothed and meshed to create high resolution textured photos, which have high similarity to the original real structure.

For this simple experiment, we generate 2 GS and 5 RS images with different motion directions during exposure. Visual features are extracted and matched beforehand on all frames. The two initial GS images and their matches are used to initialize the pipeline by extracting the standard RANSAC fundamental matrix and the following camera pose estimate. With the first poses in hand, we can triangulate the initial 3D points and use them for the RANSAC PnP on the third image. Although the method gives us a GS pose of this RS image, the estimate generally sits around the center of the motion trajectory and is a good initial guess for the following steps.

By bundle adjusting only the last frame with all fixed 3D points which reproject well on the GS prior, we can get a very good estimate of the real movement during the RS exposure. This is a well behaved problem as there are only 12 DoF and a large number of 2D to 3D correspondences constraining every image frame. After this BA step the new pose can be used to add the new visual matches to the existing tracks. Only reprojections below the given threshold are used and new 3D points are triangulated for newly created tracks. This new structural data is then jointly refined with the pose estimates on an overall BA, and then the process can be repeated adding new frames step-by-step.

In order to compare the standard GS SfM with our proposed general model, a equivalent GS pipeline can be achieved by simply changing the camera pose representation. The framework produced in this work is able to transparently switch between the different pose representations and use the correct reprojection methods where it is necessary. The entire pipeline is maintained in both models and the results can then be compared without any other influences or biases.

Figure 4.12 displays both results from GS and RS SfM pipelines. Although the GS reconstruction (c) seems to be reasonably good the camera pose estimate is off by an average of 0.78 meters and 0.045 radians. Whereas the RS SfM (b) gives poses in average only 8 millimeters and 0.0012 radians away from the ground truth (a). Furthermore, the GS SfM produces wrong structure estimate (red points in fig. 4.12c) even with all visual and geometric verification methods mentioned before.

(a) Ground truth, showing 3D structure and rolling shutter cameras

(b) RS SfM average pose estimate error of 8mm in position and 0.0012 radians in rotation

(c) GS SfM average pose estimate error of 786mm in position and 0.045 radians in rotation. Red points depict 3D structure with geometric error above 1 meter of euclidean distance to their ground truth.

Figure 4.12: Prove of concept: GS initialization and RS SfM (b) and erroneous GS SfM (c).

(a) Rolling shutter SfM against GPS/INS prior. The last cameras of each pipeline, RS and GSP/INS, are highlighted by red and black ellipses respectively.

(b) GS SfM (red ellipse) alters the aspect ration of the scene by squeezing it towards the RS readout direction.

Figure 4.13: After 100 frames, the GS reconstruction (b) shows a noticeable loss in scale leading to a shorter path even during moderated camera motions. Furthermore, the distance between the estimated and prior trajectories indicates an angular drift of around 50% larger than in the RS case (a).

4.3.1   Street View dataset

As we have seen, often GS techniques seem to work on RS data, as the resulting reconstruction and camera poses can appear to be reasonable. However, it has been previously showed that the latter result is not necessarily correct [37, 20, 27].

We run our SfM pipeline on real world data, enforcing the GS constraint, to compare the outcome with the proposed RS model and its linear camera motion assumption. Results show that in the GS case, although the reconstruction seems to be valid, a much larger drift accumulates on long sequences. Figure 4.13 demonstrates how drift and aspect ration changes may happen on GS reconstructions. The squeezing on the camera trajectory and 3D structure is predictable due to the direction of camera scanlines, as we have seen previously on figure 1.3.

4.3.2   Comparing to *Bundler SfM*

Bundler SfM by Snavely et al. [42] is a system for unordered image collections. Apart from its initial publication in 2008, it is still well known in the computer vision community for many popular articles reconstructing well known touristic landmarks from Flickr publicly hosted images. It is a mature open source system, self contained and fairly easy to use. We have chosen the latest version of Bundler as our state of the art baseline for the GS reconstructions and it will also serve to demonstrate how standard techniques behave on RS data.

The estimated pose, with its rotation and translation components, can be compared to the available ground truth in order to measure how precise the reconstruction is. For its rotation factor, the relative angles between the estimated orientation and ground truth can be used as a benchmark by computing the orientation error between each camera pair, as explained in section 4.2.1. This is similar to the methods used by [35] and [19]. However, the translation scale cannot be compared as easily as that, since the initial estimate is only correct up to a unknown scale.

The proportions between the camera positions could be used to estimate the scale, but this would also require assuming at least two camera poses to be correct in order to measure the remaining poses. This final measurement would then be biased by this assumption and actually only measure the drift from consecutive pose estimations. Fortunately, the rotation and translation factors of the camera poses are not completely independent, and data collected in the previous experiments and by [35] show a proportional average error for both of these measurements. This means a small or large value in one of the factors (rotation or translation) will indicate a proportional value on the other error factor. Therefore, benchmarking both factors would be redundant, and in this case, rotation seems to be the best candidate due to its scale independence.

A major difference between Bundler and our pipeline is that the former was not only designed exclusively for GS cameras, but it also does not make use of the given ordering during image acquisition. As we have seen, our pipeline uses the sequence information to assume that consecutive images might have a close physical position and similar orientations, and consequently are good candidates for visual matching.

On the other hand, Bundler was designed to work with unordered images from unknown sources commonly found in the Internet. Their pipeline will try

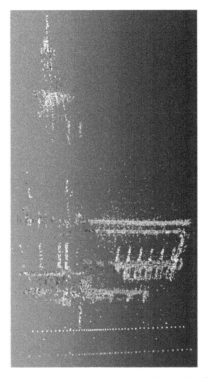

Figure 4.14: GS reconstruction made by Bundler SfM of the San Francisco City Hall's facade using Google Street View RS data. The camera centers are shown alternating in green and red. The yellow points indicates again the camera orientations. Some misplaced cameras are shown outside of the normal trajectory (bottom left) and several 3D points were triangulated far from the actual facade, despite of the geometric verification methods used in their pipeline. These points were manually colored in red and can be seen above the right wall.

to match every image against every other one in order to find the best matching pairs for the reconstruction. As it does not use the sequence of the images, repeated patterns can be easily mistaken on being from the same location and camera poses can be completely misinterpreted. Therefore, only sequences with visually unique images were used to benchmark both frameworks. Although not using the known ordering of the images might sound unfavorable, it is also an advantage for their pipeline. It will be able to create way more feature tracks

than we can do with our proposal since it is matching all images against all others
and not a limited set of last frames as we do. We could increase our number of
past frames to match, as it was mentioned before in section 3.2, but it will suffice
for the result and for the performance trade-off.

On our synthetic dataset, Bundler displayed similar results as for our GS
pipeline demonstrated in figure 4.12. Bundler showed in this case a little worst
orientation error of about 0.067 radians, which is expectable as it works in a un-
calibrated setup and only focal length information was provided to their pipeline
initialization. Moreover, it also shows similar 3D structure far from the remaining
walls, like the red points in figure 4.12(c).

Part of our Street View dataset was used to test Bundler SfM in real world RS
data. Figure 4.14 shows the reconstruction of the right half of the San Franscisco
City Hall's facade, the same dataset used in figures 4.1 and 4.13. It shows the
same scale deformations as in figure 4.13(b) and several misplaced 3D points (in
red) as on the synthetic data. In addition, a couple of cameras had wrong estimates out of the normal running path – please see cameras at the far left of the
image. Although there is no ground truth data to compare, these results visually
confirm again that a RS aware model is necessary to reconstruct RS imagery
under even smaller levels of motion.

4.4   Windowed BA

Large scale reconstructions have prohibitive memory and processing times for
most applications. However, in an incremental pipeline like ours, it is noticeable
that most estimate refinement done by the global bundle adjustment actually
happens only on the last added frames. The numerical convergence of the nonlinear squares solver tends to happen within 5 or 10 iterations due to the good
initial guess of the previous steps, with the total function cost (squared reprojection error) been reduced around a whole order of magnitude per iteration. The
estimated pose is only further altered if new feature matches are added to the
tracks contained in that specific frame.

In section 3.2 we argued that matching the 5 last frames in the sequence
should be enough to provide the pipeline with sufficient data. Additional matching could have been done to further explore the imagery for visual matches but
no guarantees can be made for the quantity and quality of these matches. Thus
the tracks in this proposed setup tend to not exceed 10 consecutive frames, as
visual features do not normally stay visible for longer than that in our datasets.
Even feature points tracked during very long frame sequences tend to not greatly

change their values after been already optimized for the past tens or even hundreds of visual constrains (2D reprojections). Consequently the BA refinement will mostly engage the last added poses and their respective tracks, and the magnitude of the correction in the remaining estimates will decrease after every new frame addition.

Nonetheless, the optimizer has to calculate the gradient of the cost function over all variables of every frame and track of the problem, increasing the computational cost proportionally. The complexity would in theory grown in $\mathcal{O}(c \cdot s)$, where c is the number of camera poses and s is the amount of 3D feature points, but because of the sparsity of the tracks it actually approximates to $\mathcal{O}(s)$, both in run-time and memory consumption. Still, reconstructions involving whole cities or even the whole world, as in the case of Google Maps, will require prohibitive amounts of resources.

A common practice is to run the BA with a sliding *window* of a certain size w in number of poses. w should be small enough so that the whole problem fits within the available memory. While the window "slides" through the sequence of frames, the current w poses are jointly optimized with all 3D points x_k viewed by the cameras within this window. In addition, every camera outside of the window that also see the same points x_k need to be considered and added as fixed parameter blocks to the nonlinear least squares problem [24, 44]. By doing so we assume the poses external to the window to be optimal and also rely on the sparsity of the tracks to save on the number of parameters, as in the worst case it would still include every existing track in the problem.

We propose here the inverse approach for the window boundary. Instead of fixing the camera poses outside of the window, we choose a window of a larger size and fix all 3D points which are also seen by any cameras external to this window. Therefore, we assume any track partially outside of the window to be already optimal and constant, and only solve for poses and tracks completely inside the running window. All other 3D points and cameras are entirely ignored as in the traditional formulation.

Our approach obviously require a larger BA window, since it would otherwise not optimize tracks with large coverage. Although this might not fit certain problems with visual features extending throughout the whole sequence, it is ideal for our incremental framework in which images are added and solved step-by-step. In this case, every 3D point is optimized for at least the same number of pipeline steps as the chosen size of window. Besides being extremely easy to implement, it considerably reduces the gradient computations per camera pose within a given window size, which allows a larger group of camera poses to be jointly optimized than in the traditional approach.

Chapter 5

Future Work

5.1 Loop Closure

Although the bundle adjustment results are optimal for a the local reprojections, there are no guarantees on the global accuracy of the reconstruction and camera trajectories. Even minor numerical errors on the local problem can accumulate to cause large drift on the large scale. This problem is more acutely seen on intersections within the camera path or between two different reconstructions being merged together, when visual components of the scene are shown in multiple distinct positions. In our specific framework, this issue can be intensified by the fact that visual features are only matched to each other on consecutive frame. Therefore, multiple visits to the same location in different times in a video might not be directly visually matched and different positions or paths might not overlap at all, if there is enough accumulated error in between. The explicit correction to this problem is typically known as *loop closure* in the robotics and computer vision communities.

Klingner et al. [24] used a 3D point *constellation* matching in order to find visual counterpart panorama pairs which already had close physical proximity. They implemented a typical RANSAC loop of the closed form method proposed by Shinji Umeyama [45] to find the relative transformation between the 3D point clouds viewed by two distinct panoramas and use this to constraint their camera poses. However, by doing so they are relying on the relation between the camera pose and the viewed 3D feature points, which is not only dependent on their 6 DoF camera pose representation but also on the relative pose of the respective scanline. In their case, the scanline position is fixed in relation to the car pose trusting on their good GPS/INS prior. Yet, the relative scanline pose might not be the same in two distinct panoramas and assuming the contrary would be again equivalent to the GS assumption of instantaneous exposure. Nonetheless, this constraint adds information to the system and had been showed to great improve their global accuracy.

A simple alternative to their approach would be to keep Umeyama's least square formulation and add it directly to the problem as another prior. This would minimize the least square distance between the points in the constellation pairs instead of the camera poses themselves. Although it will probably increase the problem's amount of residual blocks, it might be even simpler to implement.

In spite of that, a more traditional computer vision approach might be of a better fit for loop closure in our sequential pipeline. Bag-of-words [40] has been long used in the community for vision-only localization. In special, FABMAP 2.0 by Cummins et al. [10] has been used for robot relocalization and loop closure at a great scale and with enormous efficiency and precision. For every query image, FABMAP returns the most visually similar image in the database after geometric confirmation. In an incremental pipeline, the newly added recurrent images could be linked by either directly adding the confirmed matches to existing tracks, or by also using a least squares 3D distance between the new and old tracks as a weak prior as mentioned above. The first, would be a more direct, easy to implement and computationally efficient approach, while the second is a probably more flexible alternative and does not rely on FABMAP's precision.

5.2   Large scale and portability

We have seen in chapter 3 that the 2D interest points and their matches are serialized to avoid repetitive processing of these frames. Apache Thrift [41] was chosen as the serialization framework due to its simplicity and portability, but as well for its applicability as a *remote procedure call* (RPC) framework. This latter quality allows us to transparently share any serializable structure through the network or even between processes within the same machine. This permits not only the software to be better and freely organized but also enables transparent distribution of tasks inside a computer cluster or multiprocessor units. Although it has no influence on the results of our proposed camera model and pipeline, it can possible allow further usage of the framework in real world applications.

The software produced in this work was divided in two parts, in a typical client-server model. The first part (client) is responsible for image acquisition and pre-processing and the second (server) for the remaining of the pipeline. This would let us, for example, fulfill the vision of having this framework running on a mobile device, while the heavy processing is done in background in a cloud provider. Each pipeline step could be easily scaled and processed on a distributed cluster for a faster response, similar to the proposed methods [32, 47].

The only non-scalable piece of the pipeline is the track container, which would have to be refactored to allow subsectioning a large reconstruction. Currently, only the frame poses are serialized and the whole 3D structure has to be contained in the memory. Although, the used data structures have a very small footprint, this would limit the reconstruction to a couple of millions 3D points on latest computers. Dynamically loading and partially updating this structure as well as the frame poses was envisioned and should be easy to extend in the current implementation. Using a common network file system and simple inter-process synchronization, it would also allow the windowed BA to be distributed across several machines.

The feature extraction was meant to be performed on the client side as, due to its information compression nature, it will strongly reduce the streaming bandwidth to the server component. However, the feature matching process could be also done in the server side in a parallel way, as matching each individual past frame is independent from the others. Moreover, authentication and proper access control would be necessary in order to transform this prototype into a real world application.

5.3 RANSAC RS PnP

We saw in section 3.7 that robustified least square bundle adjustment can cope with Gaussian noise in practical levels but has a hard time even with low ratios of outliers. RANSAC techniques became the standard solution to handle any kind of model fitting in presence of outliers. We also saw that the standard GS RANSAC PnP can be used to initialize the RS camera pose and greatly improve the performance of our pose estimate with the proposed general camera model.

However, a much more efficient alternative to this 2-step process would be to unify them in a single RANSAC RS PnP. This should not be anything more complicated then any other RANSAC function, i.e. the minimum parametrization (a set 3D points) is randomly chosen and used on the RS BA with fixed 3D points to estimate the new camera pose with its 12 DoF as showed in equation 3.4. Yet, a better investigation is necessary to define the minimal required parametrization to work on noisy real-life data. 6 being the theoretical minimal number of 3D to 2D correspondences on noise-free data.

5.4   Alternative models

The 4th order b-spline used by Oth et al. [33] is the standard choice for a polynomial curve in trajectories with full freedom in a 3D space. It provides a smooth and differentiable model which can be easily used on BA. We strongly believe that this 6D polynomial curve could simultaneously substitute our proposed interframe linear motion and a constant velocity prior. Instead of using the costly knot optimal placement process used by Oth et al., we would suggest to limit one control point per image, assuming there is enough information in the image to constrain the curve. We also assume the camera trajectory to be smooth enough to fit the curve, which should be reasonable for good quality imagery. Although this would require a minimum number of images equivalent to the spline's minimal parametrization, it should not be an issue on larger problems.

A B-spline curve already contains a smoothing factor, which was the main incentive to introduce the motion priors mentioned on section 3.7.1. Independently of the type of B-spline chosen, the optimal control points will be selected taking in consideration reprojections on all scanlines of the whole image and its neighbors. Therefore, any change in velocity must be propagated or smoothed across all neighbors and their scanlines.

Note however, that the model would loose its frame-by-frame independence, since the scanline positions and orientations are to be determined by the global polynomial function. Therefore, simple and reusable methods like the RANSAC RS PnP proposed before are not viable.

Chapter 6

Conclusion

Although the proposed general camera model is extremely simple to implement, we could observe its capability on explaining diverse rolling shutter datasets on real and synthetic data. Its performance is above of the conventional global shutter approach even for very moderate motions. Furthermore, it could be applied on sparse ordered imagery in which no other vision-only RS model could.

The software framework built during this work shows the potential application of the current SfM techniques on nowadays standard RS cameras, even during motion. A RS bundle adjustment is capable of correcting the assumption of instantaneity used in the GS initialization and precisely estimate the motion during image exposure. No assumptions are made about the timings of those cameras or its motion pattern between consecutive frames. However, we could also see that even a very weak motion prior can improve the estimate by constraining the increased freedom of the system.

Moreover, we proposed an adaptation on current standard methods like the RANSAC PnP for a simple black-box RS aware implementation. This could then be easily integrated in any popular open source library, facilitating further development or integration in any computer vision application on RS cameras.

Bibliography

[1] S. Agarwal, K. Mierle, and Others. Ceres solver. http://ceres-solver.org.

[2] K. Atkinson. *Close Range Photogrammetry and Machine Vision.* Whittles, 1996.

[3] A. Bartoli and P. Sturm. Structure-from-motion using lines: Representation, triangulation and bundle adjustment. *Computer Vision and Image Understanding,* 100:2005, 2005.

[4] H. Bay, A. Ess, T. Tuytelaars, and L. Van Gool. Speeded-up robust features (surf). *Comput. Vis. Image Underst.,* 110(3):346–359, June 2008.

[5] S. Belongie. Rodrigues' rotation formula. http://mathworld.wolfram.com/RodriguesRotationFormula.html.

[6] G. Bradski. The opencv library. *Dr. Dobb's Journal of Software Tools,* 2000.

[7] G. Bradski and A. Kaehler. *Learning OpenCV: Computer Vision with the OpenCV Library.* O'Reilly Media, 2008.

[8] D. C. Brown. The bundle adjustment progress and prospects. In *Int. Archives Photogrammetry,* 21(3), 1976.

[9] D. Burschka and E. Mair. Direct pose estimation with a monocular camera. In *Robot Vision,* pages 440–453. Springer, 2008.

[10] M. Cummins and P. Newman. Appearance-only SLAM at large scale with FAB-MAP 2.0. *The International Journal of Robotics Research.*

[11] A. J. Davison. Real-time simultaneous localisation and mapping with a single camera. In *Proceedings of the Ninth IEEE International Conference on Computer Vision - Volume 2,* ICCV '03, pages 1403–, Washington, DC, USA, 2003. IEEE Computer Society.

[12] O. Enqvist, E. Ask, F. Kahl, and K. Åström. Robust fitting for multiple view geometry. In *Computer Vision–ECCV 2012,* pages 738–751. Springer, 2012.

[13] M. A. Fischler and R. C. Bolles. Random sample consensus: A paradigm for model fitting with applications to image analysis and automated cartography. *Communications of the ACM,* 24(6):381–395, 1981.

[14] P.-E. Forssen and E. Ringaby. Rectifying rolling shutter video from hand-held devices. In *Computer Vision and Pattern Recognition (CVPR), 2010 IEEE Conference on,* pages 507–514, June 2010.

[15] C. Forster, M. Pizzoli, and D. Scaramuzza. Svo: Fast semi-direct monocular visual odometry. In *Proc. IEEE Intl. Conf. on Robotics and Automation,* 2014.

[16] X.-S. Gao, X.-R. Hou, J. Tang, and H.-F. Cheng. Complete solution classification for the perspective-three-point problem. *IEEE Trans. Pattern Anal. Mach. Intell.*, 25(8):930–943, Aug. 2003.

[17] S. I. Granshaw. Bundle adjustment methods in engineering photogrammetry. In *The Photogrammetric Record*, 10, pages 181–207, 1980.

[18] R. Hartley and A. Zisserman. *Multiple View Geometry in Computer Vision*. Cambridge books online. Cambridge University Press, 2003.

[19] J. Hedborg, P.-E. Forssén, M. Felsberg, and E. Ringaby. Rolling shutter bundle adjustment. In *IEEE Conference on Computer Vision and Pattern Recognition*, Providence, Rhode Island, USA, June 2012. IEEE, IEEE Computer Society. http://dx.doi.org/10.1109/CVPR.2012.6247831.

[20] J. Hedborg, E. Ringaby, P.-E. Forssén, and M. Felsberg. Structure and Motion Estimation from Rolling Shutter Video. In *IEEE International Conference onComputer Vision Workshops (ICCV Workshops), 2011*, pages 17–23. IEEE Xplore, 2011.

[21] J. Heikkila and O. Silven. Calibration Procedure for Short Focal Length Off-the-Shelf CCD-Cameras. In *13th International Conference on Pattern Recognition (ICPR)*, pages 166—170, Aug. 1996.

[22] H. Jin, P. Favaro, and S. Soatto. A semi-direct approach to structure from motion. *The Visual Computer*, 19(6):377–394, 2003.

[23] A. Karpenko, D. Jacobs, J. Baek, and M. Levoy. Digital video stabilization and rolling shutter correction using gyroscopes. *Stanford CS Tech Report*, 2011.

[24] B. Klingner, D. Martin, and J. Roseborough. Street view motion-from-structure-from-motion. December 2013.

[25] H. Li, R. Hartley, and J.-h. Kim. A linear approach to motion estimation using generalized camera models. In *Computer Vision and Pattern Recognition, 2008. CVPR 2008. IEEE Conference on*, pages 1–8. IEEE, 2008.

[26] M. Li, B. H. Kim, and A. I. Mourikis. Real-time motion tracking on a cellphone using inertial sensing and a rolling-shutter camera. In *Robotics and Automation (ICRA), 2013 IEEE International Conference on*, pages 4712–4719. IEEE, 2013.

[27] F. Liu, M. Gleicher, J. Wang, H. Jin, and A. Agarwala. Subspace video stabilization. *ACM Trans. Graph.*, 30(1):4:1–4:10, Feb. 2011.

[28] D. G. Lowe. Distinctive image features from scale-invariant keypoints. *Int. J. Comput. Vision*, 60(2):91–110, Nov. 2004.

[29] L. Magerand and A. Bartoli. A generic rolling shutter camera model and its application to dynamic pose estimation. In *International Symposium on 3D Data Processing, Visualization and Transmission*, 2010.

[30] R. Mandelbaum, G. Salgian, and H. S. Sawhney. Correlation-based estimation of ego-motion and structure from motion and stereo. In *ICCV*, pages 544–550, 1999.

[31] M. Meilland, T. Drummond, and A. I. Comport. A unified rolling shutter and motion blur model for 3d visual registration. December 2013.

[32] K. Ni, D. Steedly, and F. Dellaert. Out-of-core bundle adjustment for large-scale 3D reconstruction. In *International Conference on Computer Vision (ICCV)*, Rio de Janeiro, October 2007.

[33] L. Oth, P. Furgale, L. Kneip, and R. Siegwart. Rolling shutter camera calibration. June 2013.

[34] T. Papadopoulo and O. D. Faugeras. Computing structure and motion of general 3d curves from monocular sequences of perspective images. In B. F. Buxton and R. Cipolla, editors, *ECCV (2)*, volume 1065 of *Lecture Notes in Computer Science*, pages 696–708. Springer, 1996.

[35] L. Quan and Z. Lan. Linear n-point camera pose determination. *Pattern Analysis and Machine Intelligence, IEEE Transactions on*, 21(8):774–780, 1999.

[36] E. Rublee, V. Rabaud, K. Konolige, and G. Bradski. Orb: An efficient alternative to sift or surf. In *Proceedings of the 2011 International Conference on Computer Vision*, ICCV '11, pages 2564–2571, Washington, DC, USA, 2011. IEEE Computer Society.

[37] O. Saurer, K. Koser, J.-Y. Bouguet, and M. Pollefeys. Rolling shutter stereo. December 2013.

[38] J. Shi and C. Tomasi. Good features to track. In *1994 IEEE Conference on Computer Vision and Pattern Recognition (CVPR'94)*, pages 593–600, 1994.

[39] K. Shoemake. Animating rotation with quaternion curves. In *Proceedings of the 12th Annual Conference on Computer Graphics and Interactive Techniques*, SIGGRAPH '85, pages 245–254, New York, NY, USA, 1985. ACM.

[40] J. Sivic and A. Zisserman. Video Google: A text retrieval approach to object matching in videos. In *Proceedings of the International Conference on Computer Vision*, volume 2, pages 1470–1477, Oct. 2003.

[41] M. Slee, A. Agarwal, and M. Kwiatkowski. Thrift: Scalable cross-language services implementation. *Facebook White Paper*, 5, 2007.

[42] N. Snavely, S. M. Seitz, and R. Szeliski. Modeling the world from internet photo collections. *Int. J. Comput. Vision*, 80(2):189–210, Nov. 2008.

[43] A. society for photogrammetry, remote sensing, C. C. Slama, C. Theurer, and S. W. Henriksen, editors. *Manual of photogrammetry*. Falls Church, Va. American Society of Photogrammetry, 1980.

[44] B. Triggs, P. Mclauchlan, R. Hartley, and A. Fitzgibbon. Bundle adjustment a modern synthesis. In *Vision Algorithms: Theory and Practice, LNCS*, pages 298–375. Springer Verlag, 2000.

[45] S. Umeyama. Least-squares estimation of transformation parameters between two point patterns. *IEEE Trans. Pattern Anal. Mach. Intell.*, 13(4):376–380, Apr. 1991.

[46] P. Wolf and C. Ghilani. *Adjustment computations: statistics and least squares in surveying and GIS*. Number v. 1 in 3rd Ed). John Wiley & Sons, 1997.

[47] C. Wu, S. Agarwal, B. Curless, and S. M. Seitz. Multicore bundle adjustment. In *Proceedings of the 2011 IEEE Conference on Computer Vision and Pattern Recognition*, CVPR '11, pages 3057–3064. IEEE Computer Society, 2011.

YOUR KNOWLEDGE HAS VALUE